Identity:
Truth vs Lie

Short, Simple Reminders of Who You Are in Christ

Hannah Morrell

Copyright © 2025 by Hannah Morrell

All rights reserved. No part of this publication may be reproduced, distributed, or transmitted in any form or by any means, including photocopying, recording, or other electronic or mechanical methods, without the prior written permission of the publisher, except in the case of brief quotations embodied in critical reviews and certain other noncommercial uses permitted by copyright law. For permission requests, write to the publisher at **publishing@kingdomwinds.com**.

Scripture quotations marked TPT are from The Passion Translation®. Copyright © 2017, 2018, 2020 by Passion & Fire Ministries, Inc. Used by permission. All rights reserved. ThePassionTranslation.com.

Second Edition, 2025

ISBN: 978-1-64590-075-7

Published by Kingdom Winds Publishing.
www.kingdomwinds.com
publishing@kingdomwinds.com
Printed in the United States of America.

To the God of hope who gives us Life in Jesus and a new identity.

Table of Contents

Introduction	4
Failure	6
Unloved	10
Unwanted	14
Unacceptable	18
Rejected	22
A Bother	26
Stuck	30
In Chaos	34
Governed By Fear	38
Used	42
Dirty	46
Fat and Ugly	50
Not Good Enough	54
Alone	58
Can't Get It Right	62
Left Out	66
Guilty	70
Dumb	74
Unheard	78
Betrayed	82
Abandoned	86
At Fault	90
Inferior	94
Bad Spouse	98
Bad Parent	102
A Disappointment	106

Introduction

Who are you? It's a difficult question to answer. Do you define yourself by the people around you? The experiences you've had? The job you do?

As we grow up, we generally start to form an identity based on all these things, and often, these messages shaping our identities are negative and damaging. After many years of doing pastoral counseling, I have noticed several identity messages that seem to repeat themselves in people's lives. In this book, I want to tackle the most common of these identity messages and speak truth into them, hoping you will understand your true identity and turn away from the lies.

As a follower of Jesus, I believe He has taken our old identity (or old man) and replaced it with a new identity in Him. He died on the cross and rose from the dead to new life. And now He brings us to new life as well, which means He gets to help us know our new life in Him and what's true about it.

The truth about me is whatever He says it is, whether or not it feels true in a given moment. New life in Jesus doesn't erase those damaging messages we used to shape our identities before Christ. We continue to carry around the baggage of the old identity, even though this isn't really who we are anymore. We operate as if it is true because it is our default, our "normal." The good news is that these negative identity messages are lies, but sometimes we need some repeated reminders of the truth for us to start to believe it.

My hope with this book is to give short, sweet reminders of who you are not, who you are, and who God is. I want this to be a tool for you to remember your true identity as defined by Jesus so you can live according to it, no matter what your life circumstances may be.

Truth must be repeated over and over for us to begin to believe it, especially because we tend to live out of what we feel, which can often lead us back to lies. These lies have been reverberating through our hearts and minds for years. So, I offer some time to soak in the truth of who you are. "Soaking" to me means you get as obsessive about setting your mind on the truth as you have been about obsessing over the lies that have shaped your past. Think about it like a sponge: for a sponge to soak up clean water, the dirty water must first be wrung out of it.

You can read one reminder per day, the whole book at once, or however you'd like. I tried to make each chapter short enough that even in busy times of life, you can have truth reminders at your fingertips.

Press on, my friend, to know Jesus as the Way, the Truth and the Life (John 14:6), and to truly know yourself in light of who He has made you to be.

Failure

How many times have you found yourself stewing on all the failures of your day or your life? This obsessing about stupid decisions, words spoken, and actions left undone will lead us eventually to feeling as though we are failures. It shifts from failing in behavior to having failure as an identity. There is a big difference between failing sometimes and being a failure, and beating ourselves up mentally isn't the way to try to prevent failures.

Sometimes your past compounds this feeling because someone in your life has reminded you of your failures repeatedly. If you are only told of your misses all the time, you are eventually going to take on "failure" as your identity and live accordingly. Sometimes this looks like giving up, while other times it looks like doing all the stupid things because you are expected to anyway.

Some people are considered failures already, so they rushed headlong into that identity. Why try to be something else when you are seen as failing all the time, anyway? Others fight failure and aim for perfection because they are trying to be better, but rather than others calling them failures, nothing is ever good enough in their own minds; they don't measure up to their own standards and call themselves failures. Whether the message of failure originates internally or externally, you only beat yourself up because you think you are going to do better next time.

God says that apart from Him you can do nothing (John 15:5). We nail that standard every time—nothing. But in Him, we are more than conquerors (Romans 8:37). He is the Victorious One Who has defeated sin, Satan and evil. We get to partake in that victory. God has not required us to please Him apart from His own power within us to achieve all that He wants for us. He doesn't save us and meet us at the end, hoping we did ok through life. Instead, He walks with us every step of the way as we are now in Christ, as Paul talks about more than 164 times in his letters to followers of Jesus in the New Testament. That means that we are not held to a standard that Jesus is not willing to meet through us, and we can rest as we begin to realize we are already a conqueror through Christ.

God says you are more than a conqueror through Him who loved you (Romans 8:37). A conqueror is not a failure—those identities are mutually exclusive. You may not feel this is true, but the more you fixate on being a failure, the more enmeshed in that lie you become. If, instead, you focus on the truth, even when your emotions disagree, you may find your life changing.

Today, when you start to stew and wallow in the mistakes you've made, whether real or imagined, come back to the truth that in Jesus, you are a conqueror, not a failure. Ask Him to remind you who you are, and live out of His plenty when you don't have enough.

Who you aren't: Failure

Who you are: Conqueror

Who God is: Victorious One

"Yet even in the midst of all these things, we triumph over them all, for God has made us to be more than conquerors, and his demonstrated love is our glorious victory over everything!"

—Romans 8:37, TPT

Identity: Truth vs. Lie

❦ What is distracting you today and making you feel like a failure?

❦ What voices in your life have overtly or covertly convinced you of your being a failure?

❦ Ask Jesus about what you've seen as failures in your life to get His perspective on them. Ask instead for revelation of the One Who loves you and makes you a conqueror through His Life.

Unloved

Although most parents and people around us try to love well, sometimes they miss the mark. Sometimes people are fighting their own insecurities so much that they lash out at others to make themselves feel better. Sometimes people choose to take their pain and cause pain to others. Of course, that doesn't fix the problem, and instead leaves a person feeling even less loved. We can even take the feeling of being unloved to the extreme of being completely unlovable. We think no one will ever be able to love me because I'm just too _____ or I'm just not _____.

This message is compounded by romantic interests who find someone else, friends who betray us, and other hurts that keep making us feel unloved. We eventually believe we are unlovable because we have felt unloved so many times.

The identity message of being unloved leads us to the extremes of either searching the world over for someone who might love us or closing down completely in case we are ever vulnerable to another person who can convey this message yet again. We hear over and over that we just want to find someone who will love us unconditionally, but we are very conditional beings, and humans can't provide the kind of love we really crave.

Jesus is the Lover of your soul, and He loves you to the point of dying on the cross and covering you in His blood.

Identity: Truth vs. Lie

He refers to you as His beloved. If you ever doubt the love of God for you, read Song of Songs and recognize the aching of God for you illustrated throughout that beautiful writing. God has always wanted relationship with us and was willing to do anything for us. In His overcoming love, He sacrificed His own beloved Son in order to bring restoration to that relationship with us and to provide a way out of the prison of sin.

And more than that, He puts His Spirit within us to live daily with us here in the muck and mire of life. He doesn't wait until we are cleaned up and shiny—He walks right into that mess and holds us close. This love of His just blows me away with His perseverance, faithfulness, and strength. If He loves you this much, you are not unloved. You are loved beyond what you can even comprehend. Instead of searching for the conditional human love that doesn't satisfy, try turning to Him and allowing Him to speak to you of His great love for you.

Who you aren't: Unloved

Who you are: Fiercely loved beyond comprehension

Who God is: Lover of your soul

"So now I live with the confidence that there is nothing in the universe with the power to separate us from God's love. I'm convinced that his love will triumph over death, life's troubles, fallen angels, or dark rulers in the heavens. There is nothing in our present or future circumstances that can weaken his love. There is no power above us or beneath us—no power that could ever be found in the universe that can distance us from God's passionate love, which is lavished upon us through our Lord Jesus, the Anointed One!"

—Romans 8:38–39, TPT

"The one I love calls to me: Arise my dearest. Hurry my darling. Come away with me! I have come as you have asked to draw you to my heart and lead you out. For now is the time, my beautiful one."

—Song of Songs 2:10, TPT

Identity: Truth vs. Lie

❈ What events make you feel unloved today?

❈ In your life, how has the identity message of being unloved grown into feeling unlovable?

❈ Ask Jesus to remind you of how He is the great Lover of your soul Who will never separate you from His love.

Unwanted

I have talked to several people whose parents, from the day they were born, conveyed the message they were unwanted. Some parents had wanted a girl and didn't know what to do with a boy. Some got pregnant by "accident" and felt immediate resentment toward their little one. The feeling of being unwanted stuck around, and these children have been constantly looking for someone to tell them they are wanted since then. But people are terrible at consistency.

You can begin to feel unwanted at every turn because you've internalized the overt messages you've already received. No matter what comes in a relationship, you might have so convinced yourself of your negative identity you will interpret everything through a lens of being unwanted. When you are searching for someone to want you, you will use any method you can—sex, money, power—whatever it takes for someone to want you. Of course, you can't ever know if they really want you for you, or for the trappings you wear or what you give them.

Jesus, though, wants you desperately. He wants you so much He was willing to die to have relationship with you. He doesn't reject you because He's disappointed or resentful. Instead, He died for you while you hated Him (Romans 5:8)—unrequited love in its purest form. He is the One Who pursues you again and again and again, not growing weary of reminding you of the truth of how much He likes having you close.

He is the One Who pursues to show just how wanted you are, and He will keep pursuing you to remind you of this truth. So often we turn away from His love, believing if we were chosen or wanted by a certain community or a certain person, then we would satisfy the craving deep in our souls for belonging. Community has an important place, but not as a definer of our identity. I believe that is God's place, and when we give people authority where they shouldn't have it, we jump on a horrible rollercoaster of their emotions and what we assume they think of us. Our belonging must come first in relationship with Jesus, Who never leaves, never forsakes, never abandons (Hebrews 13:5).

Who you aren't: Unwanted

Who you are: Wanted desperately

Who God is: The One Who desires relationship with you enough to die for it

> "But Christ proved God's passionate love for us by dying in in our place while we were still lost and ungodly!"
>
> —Romans 5:8, TPT

Identity: Truth vs. Lie

❀ When do you identify with feeling unwanted?

❀ What have you attempted to gain enough love from people to get rid of this identity message?

❀ Soak in the ways God has shown you His incredible love for you today.

Unacceptable

I can often feel unacceptable. I feel there are uncommunicated standards that I haven't met but still try to achieve in order to be accepted. I'm not funny enough, kind enough, pretty enough, or whatever the standard in my head is. I measure myself by so many standards of my own creation, and I always find myself lacking. It is an exercise in futility—working so hard to perform right and be what you have deemed as acceptable and yet constantly failing and feeling as though you can't measure up.

Sometimes I tell my husband how I feel I have missed the mark on something, and he reminds me that the expectation is my own, not his or anyone else's. I create standards that are higher than God's and beat myself up when I don't meet the criteria I have established in my head.

Perhaps you struggle with feeling unacceptable. Maybe you had parents who communicated you were not meeting the standard, or the expectation was unknown and thus impossible to meet. Or maybe you have a personality that automatically feels unacceptable because you tend towards perfectionism and can never live up to the expectation for yourself.

Christ says He's made me acceptable, and not because I worked really hard to meet a standard. The simple way to gain Christ's acceptance is to receive His gift of making me acceptable. It doesn't feel right because I want to earn it

Identity: Truth vs. Lie

or do something to deserve it, but put simply, I can't. I can only receive His Life, and as I am covered in His blood, I am acceptable as I am. Can you soak in that? You are acceptable. He is the only One Who can make you acceptable—not your effort, your achievement or your determination.

Sometimes this is a struggle to take in because of our pride. We want to feel as if we have earned something. But God makes it very clear in Scripture that we can't earn anything and must simply come to Him in humility. When we can put down this obsession with our own created standards, we can find rest and genuine acceptance. In recognizing our acceptance comes because God has accepted us and not through our effort or performance, we also can see that we can't lose it based on our behavior! The foundation of our acceptance is God's love, not our actions. Instead of focusing on performing, we can rest and enjoy the relationship with Jesus and full acceptance therein.

Who you aren't: Unacceptable

Who you are: Accepted

Who God is: Unconditional acceptance

"Our faith in Jesus transfers God's righteousness to us and he now declares us flawless in his eyes. This means we can now enjoy true and lasting peace with God, all because of what our Lord Jesus, the Anointed One, has done for us. Our faith guarantees us permanent access into this marvelous kindness that has given us a perfect relationship with God. What incredible joy bursts forth within us as we keep on celebrating our hope of experiencing God's glory."

—Romans 5:1–2, TPT

Identity: Truth vs. Lie

- What makes you feel unacceptable?

- What expectations have you imposed upon yourself that make you feel unacceptable?

- Meditate today on your acceptance in Jesus, understanding that you can't do anything to deserve or earn it.

Rejected

I remember a birthday party when I was in fifth grade. I invited a few close friends, and no one showed up. I sat by the window, and my hope for a party diminished more each minute as no one came. They all had good reasons, of course, but my 11-year-old brain took it all as rejection. I assumed they must all hate me and were making fun of me behind my back for even inviting them.

So many relationship issues can be read through a grid of rejection. He broke up with me because I deserve rejection, not because of his own issues. She didn't show up because she rejected me, not because she got really sick and couldn't make it. Sometimes it's true (people can be real jerks), and sometimes it's a subjective read on the situation that isn't really true. True or not, it's painful always.

The reaction to this rejection is varied. People shut down and don't want to enter into the vulnerability of another relationship, afraid they will just find another rejection there. These people might act as if they have good relationships, but really, they are very reserved as they try to keep themselves safe. Others run around trying to find someone—anyone—to accept them. They will do anything, regardless of whether they agree with it or like it, in order to avoid the rejection. Sometimes this means people end up being easily swayed by peer pressure, and they seem to be a different person with every group as they try to be everything to everyone.

The opposite of rejecting is accepting or welcoming. You don't just meet the standard now in Jesus, but He welcomes you with open arms. Think of the prodigal son returning to his father in Luke 15. The father fell on him with an embrace! He went over and above to show how welcomed, wanted, accepted and loved his son was—even when covered in pig poop.

Jesus is your welcome. He calls you through life's rejections, perceived or real, and reminds you how welcome you are with Him. You don't have to be afraid of vulnerability with Him because He loves you perfectly. Yes, there may be suffering amid a relationship with God, but suffering is never rejection from Him. As humans, we often view our circumstances as a direct reflection of our standing with God instead of taking the character of God and defining the circumstance from this truth. This may appear to be a case of semantics, but it radically shifts your understanding of God. He is Love and goes beyond anything you could imagine to welcome you into His love.

You no longer live in rejection, but are heartily welcomed and accepted. You don't have to seek acceptance in a person, but can live out of the perfect welcome in Jesus.

Who you aren't: Rejected

Who you are: Welcomed

Who God is: Your Father who welcomes you with open arms

> "Turning to his servants, the father said, "Quick, bring me the best robe, my very own robe, and I will place it on his shoulders. Bring the ring, the seal of sonship, and I will put it on his finger. And bring out the best shoes you can find for my son. Let's prepare a great feast and celebrate. For my beloved son was once dead, but now he's alive! Once he was lost, but now he is found!" And everyone celebrated with overflowing joy."
>
> —Luke 15:22–24, TPT

Identity: Truth vs. Lie

❀ In what way do you feel rejected today?

❀ How have you tried to deal with your own feeling of rejection?

❀ Ask Jesus to show you how your Heavenly Father has welcomed you with incredible grace, love, and delight.

A Bother

How often have you felt as though you were simply a bother to people? That they put up with you, but really you were in the way of what they were trying to do, and they secretly resented you for it. I know there are times I have sadly thought of my kids as a bother. I could get so much more work done if it weren't for these little loud people! But God catches me up quickly and reminds me they are never a bother to Him, or to me. He tells me that work or housekeeping are minor details in the scheme of raising small ones and that I don't want to create in them the feeling that they are a bother. My children are actually the focus of my day, not interruptions to what I should be doing.

Often, we treat people as if they are just bumps in the road of our busy lives. We can't put down our phones long enough to look them in the eye. We can't have patience with the older ones who drive or walk in front of us at a snail's pace. Our families are simply duties we must perform on the way to something more important. I hate that feeling from others, but I am often guilty of doing the same thing. Ouch.

I love the picture of Jesus with the little children, as talked about in Mark 10. He had time for them. He wasn't impatient with them, even as the disciples were trying to get them out of the way so Jesus could see more important people, or even have time by Himself. He allowed the children to come because they weren't a bother to Him.

Identity: Truth vs. Lie

Do you see that you aren't a bother to Jesus, either? He always has time for you. He is never impatient with your coming to Him again and again. He doesn't sigh and huff while listening to yet another story or question. He treasures that time with you and waits with expectation for more. I remember a friend with grown children telling me that when her kids were little, sometimes she would have to pull over her car on the side of the road to cry with the sheer joy of having them with her. That, my friend, is a good picture of how God feels about you. You are His treasure.

Who you aren't: A bother, in the way

Who you are: A treasure

Who God is: The One who treasures you beyond measure

"*Jesus gave them another parable: 'There once was a woman who had ten valuable silver coins. When she lost one of them, she swept her entire house, diligently searching every nook and cranny for that one lost coin. When she finally found it, she gathered all her friends and neighbors for a celebration, telling them, "Come and celebrate with me! I had lost my precious silver coin, but now I've found it." That's the way God responds every time one lost sinner repents and turns to him. He says to all his angels, "Let's have a joyous celebration, for the one who was lost, I have found."'*"

—Luke 15:8–10, TPT

Identity: Truth vs. Lie

❀ What times in your life have you felt like a bother?

❀ How have people communicated that you are in the way or a bother to them?

❀ Meditate on the truth—God loves and treasures you beyond what you could comprehend.

Stuck

What is it in your life that makes you feel stuck? Your job? Your family? Your mistakes? The feeling of being stuck is not necessarily defined by the truth of being stuck, but rather by the perspective of the situation. How do people in concentration camps decide to live free in their brains while their bodies are trapped? How do people in despairing poverty make their way to loving their communities rather than living in depression over the lack? There must be a choice there.

The circumstances you believe define you only do so you if you let them. Whatever it is you think keeps you stuck must be recognized as only a roadblock to be worked through, rather than a full stop that prevents you from gaining traction. The minute you believe your situation is preventing forward progress, you are denying the power of God to work in it. You are choosing to believe that this circumstance is greater than God, and you are allowing it to dictate your life.

Even Paul, while in prison, writes Philippians and talks about being free and having joy. He doesn't let prison make him feel stuck. How is that possible? Well, in Christ, we are free, and nothing can make us trapped. We are never limited to our circumstances because our God is bigger than those circumstances. We don't always have to see a way out to believe there is one. Sometimes it is about keeping your eyes and focus on the One Who is at work amid the situation, realizing the truth

Identity: Truth vs. Lie

rather than getting trapped by the feelings. Emotions aren't bad, but they should never be in charge. They should be gently and repeatedly guided to follow the truth that Jesus gives us.

The truth is that you are free, free indeed (John 8:36). So walk in the freedom. I have seen so many people decide to write a blank check to whatever they see is limiting them and sign their lives away to that thing, person or situation. Nothing defines you unless you let it. Why not let the God Who loves you define you and tell you who you are rather than listening to the lies of the evil one? Whatever it is you feel is imprisoning you, pour it out before Jesus, asking Him for freedom and the ability to see above and beyond the problem.

Who you aren't: Stuck, trapped
Who you are: Free
Who God is: The one who sets you free

"So if the Son sets you free from sin, then become a true son and be unquestionably free!"

—*John 8:36, TPT*

"At last we have freedom, for Christ has set us free! We must always cherish this truth and firmly refuse to go back into the bondage of our past."

—*Galatians 5:1, TPT*

Identity: Truth vs. Lie

❀ When do you feel stuck or trapped in your situation?

❀ What problems from your past still control you today and make you feel stuck?

❀ In focusing on your true freedom amid difficult circumstances, recognize how Jesus makes you free no matter what situation you are in right now.

In Chaos

This identity message of being out of control or in chaos is an interesting to examine because you never really were in control. It's an illusion of being in control that has been stripped from you when you feel you are in chaos. You may have grown up in a chaotic environment with an alcoholic parent who raged when they were drunk. This made you walk on eggshells whenever you were home, wondering how they would be when they got home. Or perhaps you had a parent or sibling die, and that left you feeling as if your life was in chaos. If your personality is one that likes order and to feel as if there is a plan in place, chaos and feeling out of control can be debilitating for you. It can feel as if everything is spinning, and you are left trying to hold up the world.

We are constantly looking for a safe place in this life. We want safety in finances, in careers, in relationships, in our physical bodies. We manipulate and strive to gain some sense of safety. The preparation that goes into preparing for a future event is exhausting, but it is motivated by the idea that there is a safe place we can find for ourselves in that orderly future we strive toward. Yet we are confronted almost daily with the unexpected and move right back into feeling as if we are in chaos.

I wonder, though, that even with the preparation you've done to hedge your bets, if you've ever really felt as though you were in control. Or if you may have experienced the feeling of control for a moment, only to have it ripped away by the next chaotic wave that comes your way.

Sometimes with circumstances in life, I can't explain them. I can't explain why hard things have happened. In these times, I must come back to the basics: God loves me, circumstances don't define His character, and He has a good plan for my life that He will bring about. I am not in a chaotic mess that has spun out of His control. Instead, He is weaving my life into a tapestry of beauty and preparing me for the next adventure in heaven in the best way, the way that only He can. I believe the purpose of this life is not to grasp for control, but rather to recognize God's control as we grow deeper in relationship with Jesus.

I think the identity message of being in chaos puts us in a place of believing we are failing when we feel circumstances are not how we thought they would be or how we planned. But that's not how life with Jesus is—we are not supposed to be in control or be able to tell the future. Instead, we get to walk in trust, trusting a God Who is shepherding us through each part of life, chaotic or not, into a safe spiritual reality that can't be touched by circumstance.

You are safe. You are loved. You are treasured. Soak in that.

Who you aren't: In chaos, out of control, unsafe

Who you are: Safe and loved

Who God is: The One Who knows the plans He has for you for your good

"Here's what Yahweh says to you: 'I know all about the marvelous destiny I have in store for you, a future planned out in detail. My intention is not to harm you but to surround you with peace and prosperity and to give you a beautiful future, glistening with hope.'"

—Jeremiah 29:11, TPT

Identity: Truth vs. Lie

❀ What events in your life have made you feel out of control and unsafe, like chaos surrounding you?

❀ What have you believed you were supposed to control in your life?

❀ Ask God to reveal His hand even through all of it and stand on the promise that He loves you, and His plan is for your good.

Governed by Fear

Many people with whom I talk have grown up in fear. They have been taught to be afraid of everything and operate according to that throughout adulthood. Risk is avoided at all costs because of what might happen. I notice in dealing with my own children that often my go-to is "Be careful!" I catch myself now in doing this, but it's often the overarching communication by parents (who want to keep their kids safe, of course!), and it's fear that drives our decisions. We teach our children very quickly to be careful rather than take chances.

We are afraid of so much—cancer, car accidents, getting hurt, being rejected, going broke. Forgetting who we are, we can begin to base all our life decisions on that fear, leading to closing up slowly and trying to risk nothing. It is silly, though, as our sense of control is an illusion; we really can't keep ourselves from any of these things. But we try anyway, listening to our master, Fear.

I have heard a story of how buffalo, when faced with a storm coming towards them, run directly into the storm so that they can get through it and shorten the time they must endure the driving rain and blowing wind. Most of us run away from what we are afraid of, thinking we are avoiding it or shortening it. In reality, though, facing the fear head-on and trusting God to get us through it allows us to conquer the fear instead of being held captive by it.

Identity: Truth vs. Lie

Jesus asks us to live by faith, which is the opposite of fear. When living by faith, we can be brave and do things we never dreamed we could. Our faith is in a big God Who can do supernatural things, but we often live as though we have a very small god who can't do anything. We feel we must stand up for Him somehow and make sure He doesn't get misrepresented or questioned or doubted. He doesn't need our help for any of that.

Have you noticed how many times in the Bible the phrase "Don't be afraid" or something similar is used? We have a major fear problem as humans, and God is encouraging us to move away from being controlled by fear and toward trusting Him.

Perfect love casts out fear (1 John 4:18). If I am perfectly loved and if I really believe that (which, incidentally, is a work of God in me to really believe this as well), I can do things with faith in the Lover of my soul that I would never have done in fear. I can walk forward even when things look incredibly bleak, knowing that I am not without hope. I can keep my eyes on the One Who loves perfectly instead of the waves of doubt, fear, and discouragement my circumstances bring. Perhaps it all starts by asking Him to help your unbelief and be the faith you need to take Him at His word—to stand in faith and not bend to fear.

Who you aren't: Governed by fear

Who you are: Brave because of faith in the perfectly loving One

Who God is: The perfectly loving One

"Do not yield to fear, for I am always near. Never turn your gaze from me, for I am your faithful God. I will infuse you with my strength and help you in every situation. I will hold you firmly with my victorious right hand."

—Isaiah 41:10, TPT

"For God will never give you the spirit of fear, but the Holy Spirit who gives you mighty power, love, and self-control."

—2 Timothy 1:7, TPT

Identity: Truth vs. Lie

❧ How has fear controlled you or dictated your life choices?

❧ What are your greatest fears?

❧ As you confess these fears to Jesus, ask Him to show you the courage He is giving you and how He will empower you to be who He has made you to be without being dominated by fear.

Used

I talked to a man who felt that his mother had used him as a replacement for his father in relationship. She had shared too much with him and had put him in a place inappropriate for a child. He felt used—never something we want to feel. Other kids feel used because of their accomplishments or the places their parents push them into in order to live vicariously through them. This feeling can also be a part of your life if you were abused growing up. You can feel as if you were just a body, used for someone's twisted desires.

The lie of being used often compounds into something that moves us to performance. We think we are only valuable in the sense that we are useful to someone else. So, we perform furiously and work diligently to prove our worth. The interesting thing is that the identity message of being used works hand-in-hand with the lie that you are not valuable except for what you can do. The natural reaction, then, is to work really hard to prove you are valuable—an attempt to oust the lie that you are used. How can you prove to yourself that you are not used when you still base your worth on your usefulness?

I really hate the way some Christians talk about God "using" us. It makes us sound like a hammer or a screwdriver—a tool that is used but not cared for, or given everything needed for the task at hand. Instead, the picture God gives us is the branch on the Vine (John 15). We live dependent on the Vine for life, for nutrients and sustenance, for the production of fruit. All of this is brought about naturally through us as we remain attached to the Vine. This is what we call abiding. As we remain or abide in the Vine, the natural outflow will be the promises of God and the fruit of the Spirit. We are not made to be used.

God takes usefulness out of the equation of value altogether. He says you are not to be used, but He treats you gently with respect and love. He tells you that your value is in simply being His child, not in what you do. He is a gentleman, not forcing Himself on you and making you do things. He approaches with tenderness, wooing us to Himself and showing His love along the way. I love how the writer of the Song of Songs shows us God's tender love for us. The picture here is not of a person being used and thus only valuable when needed for a purpose. Instead, it is an illustration of an extreme love for your being—for you and not what you can do.

God says you are a new creation (2 Corinthians 5:17)—you are not used or only valuable for your performance or what you can give. The old things have passed away. Let them go. Live in the identity Christ has given you rather than the lie of the old one. Celebrate the newness of your life in Him today.

Who you aren't: Used

Who you are: New creature, loved and valued

Who God is: The One Who makes you new, a gentleman

"Now, if anyone is enfolded into Christ, he has become an entirely new person. All that is related to the old order has vanished. Behold, everything is fresh and new."

—*2 Corinthians 5:17, TPT*

Identity: Truth vs. Lie

❃ How have you felt used?

❃ How has this feeling pushed you to performing or finding your worth in productivity?

❃ Take a minute to ask Jesus about who you are to Him and how He loves you completely and will not use you.

Dirty

Some of the most difficult histories for me to listen to are of those who have suffered through sexual abuse as children. I ache for kids who have dealt with this pain, especially because it leaves them feeling dirty and at fault about something they didn't choose. This is one of the great lies of the enemy—that you are to blame for the abuse done to you. You should not feel unclean because someone has chosen evil for you. This is a very hard identity message from which to separate, and it often deeply affects a person's sense of worth and choices.

I have noticed when someone feels dirty, they either try very hard to make themselves clean by living as virtuously as possible, or they throw any virtue to the wind and live as though the clean is nonexistent. Either direction lends itself to continuing to feel dirty, as the lie is so ingrained and difficult to separate from truth. Sex is something that is intended by God to be a beautiful expression of love for your mate, but the enemy twists it and makes it into a condemnation or a manipulation.

Not all who feel dirty have a history of abuse, though. You may instead struggle with feeling dirty because of things you have done and choices you have made. You can feel as though you could never be made clean because your dirt is too much. This feeling might keep you from entering productive, healthy relationships because you feel you don't deserve them. It might

Identity: Truth vs. Lie

also keep you from approaching God, believing that you need to clean yourself first but are unable to do so.

The truth is you are cleansed by the blood of the Lamb. None of the dirt from the evil you've done or that's been done to you remains. Only the feeling of it can linger as we allow it to set up residence in our minds. My friend and mentor Mike Wells used to remind people that a person's skin constantly regenerates as the old cells slough off. This means that after approximately 3 months, your whole skin has replaced itself, and not one tiny piece of your body has been touched by the evil done in the past. You are clean. You are new. You are free. Don't write a blank check to the one who did evil to you to dictate the rest of your life. Keep coming back to the truth and discard the lie that you are dirty; in Christ you are a new creation, washed clean by the blood of the lamb (Revelation 1:5), not because of anything you did or didn't do, but because Jesus says so.

Here's the other thing when it comes to the verse from 1 John below. "If we keep living" is a dependent statement, right? So, we immediately believe we need to generate something to maintain that walking in the Light, and that may bring hopelessness. But if Jesus lives in you (and He does if you have accepted His fantastic gift), then you simply need to turn to Him, and He keeps you walking in the Light. It isn't up to your willpower or strength, and it's a good thing because you can't do this on your own. Your job is choice—you must choose to turn to His Spirit within, and then He makes walking in the Light possible through His strength.

Who you aren't: Dirty

Who you are: Clean

Who God is: The Lamb of God Who provides His blood to wash us clean

"And now we are brothers and sisters in God's family because of the blood of Jesus, and he welcomes us to come into the most holy sanctuary in the heavenly realm—boldly and without hesitation. For he has dedicated a new, life-giving way for us to approach God. For just as the veil was torn in two, Jesus' body was torn open to give us free and fresh access to him! And since we now have a magnificent High Priest to welcome us into God's house, we come closer to God and approach him with an open heart, fully convinced that nothing will keep us at a distance from him. For our hearts have been sprinkled with blood to remove impurity, and we have been freed from an accusing conscience. Now we are clean, unstained, and presentable to God inside and out!"

—Hebrews 10:19–22, TPT

"This is the life-giving message we heard him share and it's still ringing in our ears. We now repeat his words to you: God is pure light. You will never find even a trace of darkness in him. If we claim that we share life with him, but keep walking in the realm of darkness, we're fooling ourselves and not living the truth. But if we keep living in the pure light that surrounds him, we share unbroken fellowship with one another, and the blood of Jesus, his Son, continually cleanses us from all sin."

—1 John 1:5–7, TPT

Identity: Truth vs. Lie

❀ When have you felt dirty?

❀ Who has convinced you in the past that you have been made dirty by their actions, or what actions of yours make you feel you are dirty?

❀ Ask Jesus for how He sees you and how dirty has no hold on you or who you are at all.

Fat and Ugly

What a daily struggle the identity message of physical imperfection is for us! It is so peculiar and yet so like the enemy to use the most superficial part of us, our body, to define the rest of us. We decide that if we don't look like a particular brand of beauty as defined by our culture, then we are inferior and unattractive. Often, our history sets us up for this as a confirmation of what we have already been made to believe. Parents, friends, and past relationships can all tell us we don't measure up physically. We are too fat, too thin, too ugly, too brunette—whatever it is. And we let it rule us. We try all sorts of different things to fix these problems, leading to more problems.

I have had models in my office, women who look like the American ideal in so many ways. At one point in my life, I would have given all my money to look like these ladies. They have the figure, the face, the whole beautiful package. And yet, even with all of that, they aren't satisfied and continue to live under the identity message of being ugly. They can point out all of their "flaws" and regurgitate the criticisms they've heard millions of times. So, the answer isn't to fix the physical issues you think you have. The answer isn't the facelift, the workout program, or the starvation routine.

Identity: Truth vs. Lie

I am not saying you shouldn't try to live in a healthy way if you'd like to do that. I am saying, though, that the motivation behind this should not be getting rid of the identity messages, or you will be disappointed. Self-help programs will not provide a way out of the lies which haunt you.

Instead, we look at what God says about us. He says He made us just as we are, and He loves us that way. This gets really tough when you are talking to a person who, since birth, has had serious differences from the cultural norm and the accompanying insecurities. But I have to stand on the truth that God made us just as He intended, and He loves us in whatever shape we're in. I think it comes down to realizing that God is not nearly as concerned about your physical appearance as you are. He recognizes it is the car in which you drive around—important enough, but not center stage, as some would have you believe.

One of my great friends was born with twisted limbs and differently formed fingers and toes. She spent the first 13 years of her life in hospitals, undergoing various surgeries and being fitted with braces to enable her to walk and go about life. I think some may look at her and feel sorry for her. But I no longer see the differences. When I look at my friend, I hear her heart, feel her beautiful soul, and watch her tenderness with others. It must be so difficult to keep walking with head held high while people stare and wonder at her. But she has decided not to allow her body to define her. And it doesn't. She is someone I hope to be like one day, choosing to focus on the pieces that matter rather than the cliché beauty standard. To me, she is very beautiful.

God says not only that He made us just the way we are, but that we are to keep our eyes on Him and not get swallowed up in analyzing ourselves. As my good friend Mike Wells used to say, "Focusing on yourself is boring!" This focus can happen whether it's negative or positive—it's still the wrong focus.

You are loved just as you are. You are treasured just as you are. You are Christ's beautiful bride, and He sees nothing but amazing love when He looks at you. That is some good news.

Who you aren't: Ugly/fat

Who you are: Beautiful and well-made

Who God is: The One Who made you beautifully

"I thank you, God, for making me so mysteriously complex! Everything you do is marvelously breathtaking. It simply amazes me to think about it! How thoroughly you know me, Lord! You even formed every bone in my body when you created me in the secret place; carefully, skillfully you shaped me from nothing to something."

—Psalm 139:14–15, TPT

"To truly know him meant letting go of everything from my past and throwing all my boasting on the garbage heap. It's all like a pile of manure to me now, so that I may be enriched in the reality of knowing

Identity: Truth vs. Lie

Jesus Christ and embrace him as Lord in all of his greatness."

—Philippians 3:8, TPT

❊ When have you believed the identity message that you are fat or ugly?

❊ Who has communicated that you are unattractive or given you these messages?

❊ Can you choose to focus on the One Who sees you as a beautiful work of His creation and loves you, rather than focusing on your flaws?

Not Good Enough

Perhaps you grew up with a parent who constantly redid whatever you had done to show you "the right way" or one who put expectations and demands on you that could never be satisfied. Or maybe a friend or romantic relationship broke up with you, implying that something about you wasn't quite up to their standard. I have also encountered many who experience the message of not being good enough because they work really hard to play a sport, get into a certain school, or do a particular job, but then get let go or passed over, anyway. Whatever you do, whatever you try, you just never can be enough for the situation or the person. This is a hopeless feeling and can lead to feeling forever doomed to spinning your wheels with no good outcome.

Whether overt or covert in their communication of this, the person (or persons) in your past has standards that are higher than God's and has passed these standards on to you. Some personalities will just dismiss this message, but many will obsess on how to be good enough, analyze what they can do to be better, and continue to beat their heads against a brick wall, hoping that they will one day be good enough. Sometimes the person with the standards is you, and your perfectionist tendencies are driving you crazy as you keep feeling that you lack. God says, though, that apart from Him, we can do nothing. So, we aren't supposed to try to be good enough. We are, instead, to recognize that we already meet the standard in Jesus.

God doesn't want our effort—He wants us to rest in Jesus' Life and have all our good works be productions of that Life. So instead of trying to prove you are good enough, you get to lay that down and start to soak in the truth that you already <u>are</u> good enough. In fact, you were worth God sending His Son to die to provide a Life with which to meet the expectation, because He knew nothing you could do ever would.

All the commands in Scripture are promises when you have the Life of Christ within providing the power to keep them. When it is up to you and your flesh, you are sunk. But in Christ, as you choose to abide in His life, you are able, and you are automatically good enough. What does abide mean? Some define it as remain, or stay. I need a picture to understand words, so my picture of abide is to turn towards my Heavenly Father and sit down in His lap, allowing myself to rest and be held by Him. This is not passivity, as choosing to turn towards Him sometimes takes everything and requires leaving behind my dependence on the flesh for a moment. At any point, I can turn back to my little energies and efforts, trying to make them enough. I must quickly realize those are not enough for the situation and come back to sit down with my Father.

Who you aren't: Not good enough

Who you are: Good enough

Who God is: The One Who makes you good enough and achieves the standard through you

> "So you must remain in life-union with me, for I remain in life-union with you. For as a branch severed from the vine will not bear fruit, so your life will be fruitless unless you live your life intimately joined to mine. I am the sprouting vine and you're my branches. As you live in union with me as your source, fruitfulness will stream from within you—but when you live separated from me you are powerless."
>
> —John 15:4–5, TPT

> "But he answered me, 'My grace is always more than enough for you, and my power finds its full expression through your weakness.' So I will celebrate my weaknesses, for when I'm weak I sense more deeply the mighty power of Christ living in me. So I'm not defeated by my weakness, but delighted! For when I feel my weakness and endure mistreatment—when I'm surrounded with troubles on every side and face persecution because of my love for Christ—I am made yet stronger. For my weakness becomes a portal to God's power."
>
> —2 Corinthians 12:9–10, TPT

Identity: Truth vs. Lie

❈ When do you struggle with the feeling as if you aren't good enough?

❈ Who is setting the standards in your life for "good enough"?

❈ Meditate on the truth that Jesus makes you good enough without your doing one thing, and allow the truth to guide your emotions.

Alone

How often as a child did you feel you were all alone in your struggle? Do you sometimes feel that way now? I remember talking to a group of women who were meeting for a small group, and one finally vocalized some of her questions and doubts. It was amazing to see the reaction in the other ladies as they realized they were not alone. I sometimes wish I could gather all the people I work with in counseling together to chat with each other so they could see that they are often struggling with similar problems and pains. The enemy loves to tell us we are the only ones who deal with some things, the only ones who are left out, the only ones who don't have anybody. That just isn't true.

Some can be surrounded by people and yet feel alone. And if you feel alone and people start to avoid you because you are disconnected, this just compounds the feeling and problem. You start to believe you are fighting these battles by yourself and no one could understand or relate to what you are going through.

I love the truth of God in this—He says He will never, ever forsake you (Hebrews 13:5). Nothing can separate you from the love of God (Romans 8:31). You are secure in Him. You are never alone. You are never fighting a battle on your own. He always shows up.

Identity: Truth vs. Lie

Sometimes the way He shows up is through other people. I don't mean you should get your love and acceptance from these people, but allow Him to work through them. God has created us to live in relationship, but often we want to isolate ourselves from people because they've hurt us or because we felt they didn't meet our needs. Of course, they weren't able to meet those needs because we were demanding of them something only God could give. So, in having love and acceptance satisfied by Jesus, we are able to be in relationship with others in a much safer way.

You are not alone. You are never separated from the love of God. He never turns His back on you. When you are tempted to believe you are alone and lost, remind yourself of the truth—He is there, He is at work, and He loves you.

Who you aren't: Alone

Who you are: Never alone

Who God is: The One Who never leaves you

"So now I live with the confidence that there is nothing in the universe with the power to separate us from God's love. I'm convinced that his love will triumph over death, life's troubles, fallen angels, or dark rulers in the heavens. There is nothing in our present or future circumstances that can weaken his love. There is no power above us or beneath us— no power that could ever be found in the universe that can distance us from God's passionate love, which is lavished upon us through our Lord Jesus, the Anointed One!"

—Romans 8:38–39, TPT

Identity: Truth vs. Lie

❀ How have you felt alone or disconnected?

❀ How have you tried to meet your need to belong primarily through messy people?

❀ Ask God to remind you that He is never going to leave you or forsake you, and get obsessive with that truth.

Can't Get It Right

Did you grow up thinking you could never get it right? That you just kept trying different angles and different maneuvers, yet it never worked out? Perhaps the expectations to which you were held were unknown or changeable. Perhaps you felt it was almost pointless to keep trying. You had become condemned to getting it wrong, no matter which way you tried to go. It's sort of one of those "damned if you do, damned if you don't" mentalities after a while.

If you are someone who likes to keep moving, it feels as though you can get no traction. If you are someone who likes to figure things out, it feels as though you can never get closure or make sense of the situation. If you are someone who loves relationship and people, you are stuck with someone who will not like you no matter how hard you try. Your frustration deepens as you keep running into a brick wall. These kinds of things leave you feeling really exhausted and angry, as though you can't do anything right, no matter how much education, experience, or help you get.

I have watched a grown man with much accomplishment be leveled by the criticism of his mother, a woman who knows nothing about the things he does but decides he is wrong regardless of her lack of knowledge of the matter. She must always have a hand in what he is doing, reminding him that he needs her and that she is always a bit disappointed in him.

I don't think any person sets out to be this kind of person, but often it is learned behavior from their past or because they think they are being helpful. But this kind of criticism rarely helps; people respond and change behavior much more when encouraged rather than criticized.

So, this is a complex identity message to sort out because Jesus tells us we really can't get it right in a lot of things, but this is an invitation to a different way of doing life. Instead of trying harder, God reminds us He is living within to make all things possible, and also that we can't try to get our acceptance from any human. When we are looking for someone to tell us we got it right, we really are telling them we want acceptance from them. And people can control you by not giving you the acceptance you want and continuing to tease you with the possibility of what you desire. They never provide the approval you want. Because they can't.

We have to set down the lie that we can't get anything right and recognize that we're asking the wrong question. It's not, "Can I ever get it right?" but "Am I not made right in Christ? I don't live under condemnation."

And the standard by which God judges "right" differs from our own. This isn't a right based on man's determination of what you should do, but it's a right that exists as a state of being made right in Christ's blood. If you can let go of trying to gain acceptance from the people around you, there's real freedom in resting in Christ's acceptance of you. In this recognition, you are not controlled by any person but are free to be exactly who you are in Jesus.

Who you aren't: Can't get it right

Who you are: Without condemnation, perfect in Jesus

Who God is: The One Who makes you perfect

"So now the case is closed. There remains no accusing voice of condemnation against those who are joined in life-union with Jesus, the Anointed One."

—Romans 8:1, TPT

Identity: Truth vs. Lie

- ❁ When have you felt as if you can't ever get it right?

- ❁ What people in your past have compounded that message in your life?

- ❁ Today, focus on how there is no condemnation in Jesus and how He makes you perfect in His Life.

Left Out

This identity message of being left out or invisible is one that hits home for me, as my whole life has rung with a feeling of not fitting in and of being an outsider. I always wanted to make people happy and to be included, and when I sensed I was left out of the group I was trying so hard to please, I felt as if my whole being was shattered. Whether it was not being invited to something to which everyone else was, working alone while everyone else had a team, or thinking I was an inside person and then coming face to face with the reality that I was an outcast—these things caused me to question my life more than anything else.

Often in talking to people, there are hurts that come back to this identity message. You weren't picked for team sports and were left standing alone while everyone else ran off to have fun. You didn't receive the acceptance letter from the college you wanted and ended up feeling stupid and left out. Maybe your parent obviously favored a sibling over you, taking them to activities and including them in things while not having time for you.

Whatever made you feel so left out, you now fight hard to be included. Your fear of missing out makes you get too little sleep, become a doormat for others and choose things that turn you into someone you are not, in hopes people will like you. You lose who God made you to be, while trying to get

Identity: Truth vs. Lie

acceptance from those around you who are a little bit crazy and really terrible at unconditional love.

Don't let crazy people tell you who you are! This comes down to feeling accepted and included. And Jesus has done the ultimate in terms of inclusion. He died for the whole world—that includes you. He offers His life to anyone who believes in Him, not just those who fit the "in" crowd. He pursues the outcasts, the rejects, the outsiders. Those are the people who realize they are sick and need a doctor. Look at how many of these people Jesus spoke to while on Earth. He hung out with prostitutes, drunks, sinners, and tax collectors—all people with whom others didn't want to be seen for fear of being rejected themselves. Jesus knew, though, that those who were left out would be the ones to recognize acceptance in Him, true acceptance that lasts and doesn't fade with the coming mood or style.

Have you ever watched a parent with a child they adore? How they watch them and smile at their antics and engross themselves in their stories? How they love spending time with them, regardless of what they are doing? That is a great picture of God's Father-love for you. He dotes on you. He calls you His beloved child. He always has time for you and delights in you.

In Christ, you are included, perfectly loved just as you are, and never on the outside looking in. You can find rest rather than the striving that's been your whole life—trying to find the inside of a group somewhere who would love you. And when you find rest in Jesus, you recognize that no one can control you in this anymore because they don't define belonging for you. You matter. You belong. You are not invisible. You are His beloved child. Nothing anyone else says or does can change that.

Who you aren't: Left out, excluded, invisible, outcast

Who you are: Always seen, beloved child of God, included

Who God is: Your loving Father Who never sees you as on the outside

"Later, Jesus and his disciples went to have a meal with Levi. Among the guests in Levi's home were many tax collectors and notable sinners sharing a meal with Jesus, for there were many kinds of people who followed him. But when the religious scholars and the Pharisees found out that Jesus was keeping company and dining with sinners and tax collectors, they were indignant. So they approached Jesus' disciples and said to them, 'Why is it that someone like Jesus defiles himself by eating with sinners and tax collectors?' But when Jesus overheard their complaint, he said to them, 'Who goes to the doctor for a cure? Those who are well or those who are sick? I have not come to call the "righteous" but those who are sinners and bring them to repentance.'"

—Mark 2:15–17, TPT

"But those who embraced him and took hold of his name he gave authority to become the children of God!"

—John 1:12, TPT

Identity: Truth vs. Lie

❧ When have you felt left out, as if you are an outcast and everyone else is included?

❧ What groups of people have you tried to find belonging and inclusion within?

❧ Spend some time today thanking God that He always sees you and always includes you.

Guilty

Think about the thing for which you feel the most guilt. Where does remembering that take you? Probably a pretty dark place. I can still vividly remember a former friend's face when I criticized her for something (because I was jealous) many years ago. She looked as though I had just punched her. And I hated myself for saying it. I even looked her up twenty years later and apologized for it when I found a way to do so. There is considerable guilt there if I allow it.

What does the enemy repeatedly bring up in your mind to send you to that place of being drowned in guilt? Does he remind you of the thing you should have done and didn't? Or the thing you did and hurt someone deeply? I talk to people in deep guilt over bullying, abortions, rejecting people, not stepping in to help someone they suspected was being hurt, and on and on it goes. The guilt festers in the heart, raining on every good thing that comes as it reminds you that you shouldn't be happy because you did this thing. Satan is the accuser, and he wants to have control over us. Jesus won't allow it.

Can you see how much of a lie false guilt is? It is one of the greatest tools of the enemy to stagnate us and keep us stuck. I'm not saying for a second that we've never done anything wrong. I am saying, though, that Jesus died for all that sin, and it is gone and forgiven. When we revisit that place over and over, we are cheapening Jesus' sacrifice—making it seem as if it were pointless. And we are trying to make ourselves do better in the future by trying really hard in our own strength.

Here's the thing, though. If it's true that only Christ's life enables us to do any good thing, then our flesh is not capable of self-improvement, no matter how many different ways you beat it up. Instead, we are to turn more and more to the Spirit and live out of His Source rather than our own strength. If we try to chastise ourselves for doing something dumb, we are trying to strengthen that flesh and make it do something it can't.

Guilt must be put down and surrendered, for it isn't defining you. You are redeemed, bought by the blood of the Lamb, and no longer condemned. Don't choose to live under guilt any more. Recognize Jesus has bought you out of that sin, and you are set free to walk forward with no guilt dragging behind you and slowing you down. There is no condemnation, no false guilt, no reason to keep going back there.

Who you aren't: Guilty, condemned

Who you are: No longer condemned

Who God is: The One Who takes your sin and through sacrifice offers a way out

> "You may discipline us for our many sins, but never as much as we really deserve. Nor do you get even with us for what we've done. Higher than the highest heavens—that's how high your tender mercy extends! Greater than the grandeur of heaven above is the greatness of your loyal love, towering over all who fear you and bow down before you! Farther than from a sunrise to sunset—that's how far you've removed our guilt from us. The same way a loving father feels toward his children—that's but a sample of your tender feelings toward us, your beloved children, who live in awe of you."
>
> —Psalm 103:10–13, TPT

> "Since we are now joined to Christ, we have been given the treasures of redemption by his blood—the total cancellation of our sins—all because of the cascading riches of his grace. This superabundant grace is already powerfully working in us, releasing all forms of wisdom and practical understanding."
>
> —Ephesians 1:7–8, TPT

Identity: Truth vs. Lie

❊ What makes you feel guilty today?

❊ How does guilt control you and condemn you?

❊ Meditate on the fact that in Christ your sin and guilt are taken and covered in His blood. Ask God for Him to reveal to you the freedom that comes when you are no longer controlled by guilt.

Dumb

During college, I worked part-time in a high school classroom for emotionally disturbed students. One message these kids had received countless times was that they were stupid. My own husband struggled through a learning disability and worked very hard to get through school. His message to himself was always that he was too dumb to figure it out because reading was difficult. And yet he is one of the smartest guys I know.

Was there something in your past that reflected this message to you? Were you told overtly or covertly that you were just too dumb to figure it out? Did you fail some things in school? Did you have to drop out of something because it was too hard, or did you end up listening to people who hurt you over and over and led you to believe you were just too stupid to do it right?

This is another identity message where Christ's Life changes our identity from what feels true about us naturally to what our potential in Jesus is. God refers to us as His sheep—not exactly a compliment in terms of intelligence. But the best thing about being sheep is that sheep have a shepherd. Our Shepherd has wisdom that is way beyond what we could come up with, so when we are in Christ, we are the smartest we could ever be. We also have ability we would never have on our own because He can be all that we need for things we couldn't do otherwise.

Identity: Truth vs. Lie

This means I'm off the hook for getting it all right in my head. If there's a decision that needs to be made, I trust Him for the wisdom to decide well. If there's something I want to understand, I ask Him for that revelation. Some of it He doesn't give me right now, but He's the one who has all knowledge and wisdom, so we trust Him to give it when we need it.

When we humbly acknowledge His intelligence being way above ours, we can access that wisdom and are not limited to our own knowledge. We can also see His wisdom at work in other people as He brings those around us who complement our weakness with their strength. I'm not too bright in some things, and I ask for help from those who are. This is another way God provides wisdom.

When we trust God's wisdom and His willingness to speak to us, we don't have to be the smartest person in the room, or to treat ourselves as though we can't do things because we aren't smart enough. We have access to the Wisdom of the Ages and don't have to live an identity message of "stupid" ever again.

Who you aren't: Dumb

Who you are: Wise in Jesus

Who God is: The Wisdom of the Ages

"For we did not receive the spirit of this world system but the Spirit of God, so that we might come to understand and experience all that grace has lavished upon us. And we articulate these realities with the words imparted to us by the Spirit and not with the words taught by human wisdom. We join together Spirit-revealed truths with Spirit-revealed words."

—1 Corinthians 2:12–13, TPT

Identity: Truth vs. Lie

❀ Can you identify some times you have felt dumb?

❀ Is your expectation of yourself to know it all and depend on yourself for wisdom for every circumstance?

❀ Meditate on the exciting fact that you have the Wisdom of the Ages through Jesus' Life in you.

Unheard

Do you sometimes feel that you chatter on and no one listens? No one cares what you have to say, and you feel as though you are just talking to the air. Feeling unheard leads us to feel unvalued, as if no one cares about what is going on with you or what you might contribute to the conversation. You begin to feel you just don't matter, that you could disappear, and no one would even care.

Was there something that was always more important than you were when you were a child? Maybe your parents shushed you because they were working or their friends were more important. Or maybe you tried to tell someone about a hard circumstance in your life, and no one bothered to take time to listen. Or they argued with you about what you were experiencing, telling you that you were wrong for feeling as you did.

I have a picture in my head that I use whenever I feel distraught and have lost focus. It comes from the passage below about approaching the throne of Grace with boldness. It is walking into a room with my gracious, kind Heavenly Father sitting on a chair and crawling up into His lap to tell Him about everything. And He holds me and listens intently, not distracted by a million other things He needs to do, but really makes me the important thing in that moment. And He lets me chatter for a while and then reminds me of His truth, and I am at peace.

Identity: Truth vs. Lie

I also think of the passage in Matthew 19 where Jesus tells the disciples to let the children come to Him, that He's not too busy with other things for them. Jesus is never too busy to hear you. And more than that, He hears your heart and not just your words. How often do I wish that people could see my heart when my words don't tell the real tale? He gently reminds me of Who He is and how He empowers me to do everything He asks of me. But I am not following a brash Shepherd who doesn't even know my name—He is individually involved in my life and hears me, even the unspoken desires of my heart.

Who you aren't: Unheard

Who you are: Heard, Known

Who God is: The Father Who listens

"Then they brought little children to Jesus so that he would lay his hands on them, bless them, and pray for them. But the disciples scolded those who brought the children, saying, 'Don't bother him with this now!' Jesus overheard them and said, 'I want little children to come to me, so never interfere with them when they want to come, for heaven's kingdom realm is composed of beloved ones like these! Listen to this truth: No one will enter the kingdom realm of heaven unless he becomes like one of these!'"

—Matthew 19:13–14, TPT

"And in a similar way, the Holy Spirit takes hold of us in our human frailty to empower us in our weakness. For example, at times we don't even know how to pray, or know the best things to ask for. But the Holy Spirit rises up within us to super-intercede on our behalf, pleading to God with emotional sighs too deep for words. God, the searcher of the heart, knows fully our longings, yet he also understands the desires of the Spirit, because the Holy Spirit passionately pleads before God for us, his holy ones, in perfect harmony with God's plan and our destiny."

—Romans 8:26–27, TPT

Identity: Truth vs. Lie

> "He understands humanity, for as a man, our magnificent King-Priest was tempted in every way just as we are, and conquered sin. So now we draw near freely and boldly to where grace is enthroned, to receive mercy's kiss and discover the grace we urgently need to strengthen us in our time of weakness."
>
> —Hebrews 4:15–16, TPT

- When have you felt unheard in your current or past circumstance?

- How have you quit using your voice because it feels like no one cares to listen?

- Take some time to talk to our kind Shepherd Who always listens, never grows impatient, and knows you inside and out.

Betrayed

How often have you experienced the back-stabbing pain of betrayal? Sometimes it's a childhood betrayal of a father who started a new family and left you in the dust. Other times, it's a romantic relationship where someone cheated on you. Or a friendship you thought you had but later discovered the so-called friend was bad-mouthing you to others.

We make our way through life looking for someone who won't let us down, someone to be faithful. We hope that our wedding vows will do it, but that isn't a guarantee either. We just want someone who won't turn their back on us and leave us feeling like a shell of a person. And when the people we love betray us, we internalize the message that somehow we're unworthy of their faithfulness; we take up the identity of betrayed, and somehow we feel we deserve it.

We can talk about how people who betray are often struggling with their own insecurities (which is usually true), but this doesn't alleviate the pain of a betrayal, especially by someone very close to us. Betrayal is a different grief than a death, as the betrayer is still walking around to remind you of the loss and to continue the message of your being unworthy of faithfulness.

A faithful friend is worth more than gold, but every human messes up. The only One we can rely on to be truly faithful all the time is God. He is the One Who came to us while we were still His enemy and died for us, something few would do for a friend. He is the One Who remains faithful even when we are faithless. He is the One Who comes back to us again and again regardless of how we betray Him. He is the One Who loves us even when we stab Him in the back and spit in His face. He is the One Who chooses to cover our faithlessness in the blood of His Son, seeing us as children who will always, always, always be loved by Him.

This faithfulness amazes me daily. It is a part of God's character and will never change. His faithfulness is something we can rely on. If He won't ever turn His back on me, even during the times that it feels like He has, I can walk forward with a bravado that I couldn't have otherwise because when others are faithless, God is faithful.

We want to shy away from people after a betrayal. Jesus went to the cross to bear sin that wasn't His. He was betrayed by Judas, by Peter, by all who should have stood up for Him. Yet, He allowed Himself to be vulnerable to them because He trusted the Faithful One and knew that no human betrayal could end Him. Betrayals hurt, but they don't have to be the end. If we will entrust ourselves to the Faithful One above and beyond any other, we can endure the betrayal of those around us. In light of God's faithfulness, betrayal of others is part of our story, but it doesn't define who we are.

Who you aren't: Betrayed

Who you are: Faithfully loved

Who God is: The Faithful One

"God is not a man, that He should lie, nor a son of man, that He should repent; has He said, and will He not do it? Or has He spoken, and will He not make it good?"

—Numbers 23:19, NASB

"So now wrap your heart tightly around the hope that lives within us, knowing that God always keeps his promises!"

—Hebrews 10:23, TPT

Identity: Truth vs. Lie

✤ How have you felt betrayed?

✤ Does the feeling linger often in fear and anticipation of the next betrayal, causing you to avoid people or keep them at a distance?

✤ Meditate on the amazing faithfulness of God in your life regardless of what others do and the firm foundation His faithfulness provides.

Abandoned

The message of abandonment can come from a slew of problems and hurts. Maybe being left behind in a store accidentally, having a parent choose to move away because their new job was more important, or being given up by biological parents to the foster system (even if you realize logically that it was the right decision for them). These people have communicated you weren't worth remembering, sacrificing comfort, or sticking around. This is such a painful message.

Because you might feel abandoned already by others, you do your utmost to make sure it doesn't happen again. You cling to those who are hopefully going to stick with you and manipulate, coerce, and charm them into staying. But sometimes they leave, too, and you are right back in that place of not being worth their staying. You might say you blame them for the leaving, but really you often believe something about yourself has made them run away.

"[God] will not desert you or abandon you" (Deuteronomy 31:6, NASB). If you have an identity consumed by abandonment, please soak in these words of God for you. You may not believe them yet, and that's ok. But soak in them and allow Him to prove them true. I can't tell you how many times I've abandoned my God. I've walked away and told Him I wanted nothing to do with Him. I've lashed out in anger and confusion at the things He's allowed. I've gone into bitterness over the choices others have made for which I want to blame Him. And yet, even in the face of outright derision, He has never abandoned me. He has never walked away.

Sometimes it might feel as though He's gone, but the truth is, He is always there, always loving, and always at work, even if quietly and underground where we don't notice. When life doesn't make sense and you feel as though it's all falling apart, go back to the One who never leaves or forsakes, reminding yourself of the truth of this over and over. It doesn't mean that life doesn't hurt sometimes, but it allows a way through the pain.

You are never abandoned, never forsaken, never left behind.

Who you aren't: Abandoned

Who you are: Kept, claimed, wanted

Who God is: The One Who never leaves or forsakes

"Be strong and courageous, do not be afraid or in dread of them, for the Lord your God is the One who is going with you. He will not desert you or abandon you."

—Deuteronomy 31:6, NASB

"So now I live with the confidence that there is nothing in the universe with the power to separate us from God's love. I'm convinced that his love will triumph over death, life's troubles, fallen angels, or dark rulers in the heavens. There is nothing in our present or future circumstances that can weaken his love. There is no power above us or beneath us— no power that could ever be found in the universe that can distance us from God's passionate love, which is lavished upon us through our Lord Jesus, the Anointed One!"

—Romans 8:38–39, TPT

Identity: Truth vs. Lie

❀ How has your past made you feel abandoned?

❀ How do you try to prevent abandonment in your life today?

❀ Ask God to show you His consistency in showing up through your life as He continues to want and keep you.

At Fault

When I was a kid, I hated going to the bathroom. I thought it was a huge waste of time and would push the limit on how long I could hold it. One time in school, I was sitting on the reading rug when someone made me laugh really hard, and I wet my pants. It was so embarrassing, and I remember the kids around me laughing when I got up and there was a little spot on the carpet from my accident.

Looking back at that moment, I want to beat up on my little 5-year-old brain and lay blame for the embarrassment. But our childhood brains are not developed enough to really process through these things—that's how we learn. I would never look at a small child today and blame them for not knowing how this works. Sometimes little ones just forget they have to go potty. But we blame ourselves often for things that happened to us as children. Or we feel manipulated into things and decide we will always be manipulated because we are just too gullible.

I was talking to a lady the other day who felt duped, as if she had been too gullible and had fallen for something someone had said. She felt as though the hurts she had received as a child could all be traced back to her own faulty reasoning or lack of knowledge.

Why didn't you just ignore those kids making fun of you? Why didn't you go tell your parents about the kid touching you in places they shouldn't have? Why did you let someone treat you that way?

These questions lay blame on the child rather than recognizing that people do evil things to others, and sometimes we don't respond well because just don't yet have the reasoning of an adult. Sometimes, even as adults, we still take blame for choices we didn't make.

God doesn't place blame because He has taken the effects of sin on Himself already. He recognizes that sometimes you don't choose things, but they choose you. And that doesn't make it your fault. Blaming yourself does no good thing for your identity, for in Christ, you are not at fault. You are free from beating yourself up because you are free from sin. This doesn't mean you don't mess up sometimes, but it does change how you deal with this feeling of being at fault.

Who you aren't: At fault, manipulated

Who you are: Blameless and wise in Christ

Who God is: The One Who makes you blameless in Jesus' blood and provides the wisdom we need

"Every spiritual blessing in the heavenly realm has already been lavished upon us as a love gift from our wonderful heavenly Father, the Father of our Lord Jesus—all because he sees us wrapped into Christ. This is why we celebrate him with all our hearts! And in love he chose us before he laid the foundation of the universe! Because of his great love, he ordained us, so that we would be seen as holy in his eyes with an unstained innocence."

—Ephesians 1:3–4, *TPT*

Identity: Truth vs. Lie

- What events in your life leave you feeling at fault or manipulated?

- How do you take responsibility or blame for choices you didn't make? Or refuse to accept God's forgiveness for the choices you did make?

- Contemplate how Jesus makes you blameless and gives you wisdom beyond what you have naturally. His Life allows us to move forward without that judgment anymore, so start to give Him all the blame and responsibility you have taken on yourself.

Inferior

Do you sometimes struggle with feeling inferior as you compare your life to others around you? This can start in childhood when you don't have the cool clothes, the right friends, or the perfect boyfriend/girlfriend. You might feel as though everyone around you has all this great stuff, and you don't. You are less than, inferior. Maybe you grew up in poverty, starving and neglected as you faced each day with fear for survival.

I think the tendency for dealing with this identity message is to make yourself rich, powerful, or find a cute spouse in order to get rid of feeling inferior. You want to walk around feeling better than everyone else. But even with all of this, once you achieve what you thought would work, you still have to have more or do better. It just isn't enough.

Feeling superior doesn't satisfy, and the feeling of inferiority still plagues you. The comparisons can keep coming. You might try making someone else feel bad to feel better about yourself, but this also doesn't help the feeling of being inferior go away.

You are called a daughter or son of the King (John 1:12–13). That makes you a prince or princess. But that doesn't seem enough because we let our feelings dictate who we think we are. So, if we feel inferior, we must be. But God says the truth is that we are exactly where we need to be because He makes it so.

Identity: Truth vs. Lie

We have to take our eyes off the people around us and what they have and put them back on Jesus, the One Who gives us exactly what we need. I know it would be nice if He thought I needed a nicer car or a bunch more money, but really, He knows what I NEED. And He knows what is best for me.

The stuff I have doesn't for one minute determine who I am. I am not inferior—I am valued just as I am. Stuff doesn't make me better or worse. It is just stuff. And it passes. The truth of God determines who I am—what is true about Jesus is true about me, because His Life is within me.

So, I am treasured. Valued. Prized. I am not determined by the things I have or have not, and my social standing is meaningless. I am the daughter of the Most High God Who loves me regardless of how inferior I seem to others on Earth. In fact, He says that the least will be greatest and the last first (Matthew 20:16). He takes the world's economy and flips it on its head.

I don't have to prove superiority either. I am an earthen vessel which contains a treasure beyond gold (2 Corinthians 4:7). Jesus lives in me, and I am valued just as He is. Amazing stuff!

Who you aren't: Inferior

Who you are: Treasured

Who God is: The One Who gives me meaning

"But those who embraced him and took hold of his name he gave authority to become the children of God! He was not born by the joining of human parents or from natural means, or by a man's desire, but he was born of God. And so the Living Expression became a man and lived among us! We gazed upon his glory, the glory of the One and Only who came from the Father overflowing with tender mercy and truth!"

—John 1:12–13, TPT

"Now you can understand what I meant when I said that the first will end up last and the last will end up being first."

—Matthew 20:16a, TPT

Identity: Truth vs. Lie

❀ When do you fight feeling inferior?

❀ What have you tried to do to get rid of the identity message of inferiority?

❀ Ask God to reveal the incredible worth that God gives you as He pursues you to the ends of the earth, and what being treasured really looks like.

Bad Spouse

If you have been married at some point, the enemy wants to tell you that you have been, and will continue to be, a terrible spouse. He brings up all the things you've done wrong (and I'm not saying you've been perfect through the marriage, but my guess is you haven't done <u>everything</u> wrong) and beats you up for them.

Of course, when we think of the ways we have messed up in relationship, we like to accuse the other party of all the things they've done wrong so we look better. We try to justify our screw-ups. We don't do very well. It's the wrong approach.

If you are in Christ, you can do marriage in a way that you never could before. You can take all the ways you've hurt your mate and apologize in a humility that comes only from Jesus. This doesn't then allow you to justify criticizing them for their own times of hurting you, but it means you can move into forgiveness with them as well. This is only possible in the Life of Christ, as sometimes it seems that you could never forgive the wrongs a person has done to you.

God makes it possible to forgive and to love the unlovable. You don't get out of loving your mate because they aren't acting appropriately. Of course, I am not talking about abuse here. But when your mate offends you and is sometimes in a bad mood and leaves their socks everywhere around the house, you get to choose to move into the Spirit and love them. Not because they deserve it, but because you have a Love in Christ that supersedes all the love you could ever have for them.

Often, I want to stay in this place of obsessing over all the things my husband has done wrong. It's a double standard, and it encourages me to move into an ever-descending spiral of bitterness. Jesus reminds me of how He's forgiven me and taken all of my junk, and He can do the same with my husband. Who am I to hold all these things against my husband and decide to live in judgment when God doesn't do that with me?

In Christ, I am a loving wife who holds no record of wrongs, doesn't seek revenge, is patient, kind, etc. This is the potential of Jesus' Life in me. All the things that are true about love in 1 Corinthians 13 are possible when Jesus lives through me. That is a miracle for every day!

Who you aren't: A bad wife/husband (if married at some point)

Who you are: A loving wife/husband

Who God is: The One Who provides the love for the spouse

"Love is large and incredibly patient. Love is gentle and consistently kind to all. It refuses to be jealous when blessing comes to someone else. Love does not brag about one's achievements nor inflate its own importance. Love does not traffic in shame and disrespect, nor selfishly seek its own honor. Love is not easily irritated or quick to take offense. Love joyfully celebrates honesty and finds no delight in what is wrong. Love is a safe place of shelter, for it never stops believing the best for others. Love never takes failure as defeat, for it never gives up."

—1 Corinthians 13:4–7, TPT

Identity: Truth vs. Lie

❈ When do you feel as if you are failing in your marriage?

❈ How have you harbored a list of wrongs done by your spouse to justify your not loving them?

❈ Ask Jesus to be your love for your spouse, realizing that in Christ you have a love that surpasses anything you could muster on your own.

Bad Parent

For a long time, I didn't want to have kids because I was pretty sure I was going to screw them up. The truth is, I know I mess up with them even after finally deciding to have them. My good friend and mentor, Mike Wells, used to tell me that we can be terrible parents 5% of the time and assume we are terrible 100% of the time. We will all have times of doing it wrong, but if you are trying to love the kids and be supportive, that means you aren't doing it wrong all the time.

When you grow up with the message that you are probably going to be a bad parent or find reasons to support this message as you get older, this can be a tough thing to fight through. You begin by believing you are doing it wrong and continue to feel this way throughout. Here's the thing—without Jesus, you are going to mess up, but in Him you can parent in a way you've never dreamed.

I don't think there is a way to "always" parent. In fact, I think parenting requires a relationship with God that keeps us coming back to Him over and over. Sometimes a situation requires one thing, and other times it requires a completely different response. You need a relationship with your Heavenly Father to know how to parent a child in each circumstance and according to their individuality.

So, in Christ, you are not a bad parent. You actually can meet your children where they are in a way you can't by yourself. In Christ, you depend on Him for your wisdom and love for these kids God's given you. That's a good thing. When you depend on Him, you are accessing the power of God to do good things in these kids' lives.

Kids push us to Jesus in a way few other relationships do, especially when we feel as if we are failing. But we listen to the Spirit with our kids as much as possible and let Him deal with the rest. I have seen kids come out of incredibly messed up homes and make great choices to change their outlook for the better, and I have seen kids come out of great homes and make poor choices to drown themselves in hard things. At the end of the day, it comes down to the child's choice and the work of God in their lives.

You have to trust God with the children He's given you, knowing that often He will bring into their lives the kinds of hard things that brought you to Him. As parents, we want to prevent these experiences because they hurt and are difficult to bear. But these experiences are worthwhile in that they bring our children to Jesus.

One other thing to mention is those whose children are already with Jesus, who moved into heaven before we did. Even though our children have died and are no longer part of our daily lives, we can definitely still label ourselves as a bad parent and take the blame for their deaths. Grieving these children is important, and so is asking Jesus to show you how He holds them now, knowing they are in the safest place they possibly could be with Him. Grief never leaves us, but it can shift from feeling as though we will drown in it to eventually becoming part of what motivates us forward and onward in relationships and life.

Who you aren't: Bad parent

Who you are: A dependent-on-Jesus parent

Who God is: The great Father Who meets you in all your parenting situations.

> *"I know what it means to lack, and I know what it means to experience overwhelming abundance. For I'm trained in the secret of overcoming all things, whether in fullness or in hunger. And I find that the strength of Christ's explosive power infuses me to conquer every difficulty."*
>
> —Philippians 4:12–13, TPT

Identity: Truth vs. Lie

❀ When do you feel as if you are failing as a parent?

❀ How have you taken responsibility for your children's choices and tried to control the outcome by beating yourself up?

❀ Ask God to show you how He, as our Heavenly Father, can be enough for any parenting situation and never leaves you to figure it out on your own.

A Disappointment

I read a biography of Hudson Taylor when I was about 11, and I remember thinking about being a missionary to China. I was pretty sure God was going to make me do this because it was the last place I wanted to go. And wasn't that the Christian life? How miserable can God make you? Nothing against China, of course, but I had no desire to live that life. My lack of desire made me feel like a giant disappointment to God. I made a lot of assumptions about what He wanted and felt I was failing on all counts.

I have also wrestled with feeling like a disappointment to my husband, my friends, my parents and my friends. This hasn't necessarily been communicated by them, but when I feel I'm not meeting the expectations I assume they have for me, I can feel like I'm failing all the time. Sometimes I don't meet the expectations and can disappoint people in my life, but that doesn't mean I should take on the identity message of disappointment.

Have you ever felt as if you are disappointing God? As if you have screwed up your life beyond repair? As if you have made all the wrong choices and now have to live in this permanent state of hanging your head around God while He points His finger at you and tells you all the ways you have missed His expectations?

Identity: Truth vs. Lie

Good news! His expectations are pretty simple. He says "Apart from Me you can do nothing" (John 15:5, NASB). We hit nothing every time. What kind of freedom would you find if you realized that God expects you to get it wrong without Him? What if you recognized that only in Him could you do all the things you thought He expected of you? What if you came to terms with releasing that pressure?

You are not a disappointment to God. You have not failed out of life. You are His beloved child, and He is well-pleased with you as you live out of the Life He has given you. And, if you haven't been accessing all that you have in His Life within you, today is a great day to start. You will then begin to see the commands of God as promises rather than demands, for He has provided the power to achieve them rather than just leaving you to figure it out. He meets all your needs in Christ Jesus and sees you as you truly are—not as you think you are. God actually delights in you!

As you soak more and more in your true identity in Christ, I hope you will be drawn to the realization of the truth versus the lies in your heart and see the truth overpower the lies that wish to drown you. You don't have to live out of the old identity that threatens to control you, regardless of how it makes you feel. You are free, loved, and treasured.

Who you aren't: A disappointment to God

Who you are: Beloved child. Delight

Who God is: The One Who provides all you need to live the life He asks of you

> "Yahweh, your God, is inside you. He is the Warrior-Savior who takes such delight in you that it will make him leap for joy and shout with great gladness. Yes, he will soothe you with his love, He will sing over you his song of praise."
>
> —Zephaniah 3:17, TPT

> "So you must remain in life-union with me, for I remain in life-union with you. For as a branch severed from the vine will not bear fruit, so your life will be fruitless unless you live your life intimately joined to mine. I am the sprouting vine and you're my branches. As you live in union with me as your source, fruitfulness will stream from within you—but when you live separated from me you are powerless."
>
> —John 15:4–5, TPT

Identity: Truth vs. Lie

❊ When do you think of yourself as disappointing God?

❊ When do you feel like a disappointment to others in your life?

❊ Soak in how beloved you are, how God delights in you, and how you have the Life of Jesus to live out all the promises He gives. Celebrate that it isn't up to you because He does the work through you.

www.ingramcontent.com/pod-product-compliance
Lightning Source LLC
Chambersburg PA
CBHW072205100526
44589CB00015B/2379